FULLY COMMITTED

BY BECKY MODE

Based on characters created
by Becky Mode and Mark Setlock

★

DRAMATISTS
PLAY SERVICE
INC.

FULLY COMMITTED
Copyright © 1995, 2001, Becky Mode

All Rights Reserved

SPECIAL NOTE

The Off-Broadway Production of "Fully Committed" was produced by David Stone, Adam Pascal, Jesse L. Martin and Susan Quint Gallin.

"Fully Committed" received its World Premiere
September 1999 at the Vineyard Theatre, New York City.

Originally developed at the Adirondack Theatre Festival,
Glens Falls, New York, in June 1998
(Martha Banta, Artistic Director; David Turner, Producing Director).

FULLY COMMITTED was originally developed at the Adirondack Theatre Festival (Martha Banta, Artistic Director; David Turner, Producing Director), Glens Falls, NY, in June 1998. It was directed by Philip Shneidman; the lighting design was by Jamie Pusateri; and the sound design was by Douglas Graves. The actor was Mark Setlock.

FULLY COMMITTED received its world premiere in September 1999 at the Vineyard Theatre (Douglas Aibel, Artistic Director; Barbara Zinn Krieger, Executive Director; Jeffrey Solis, Managing Director) in New York City. It was directed by Nicholas Martin; the set design was by James Noone; the lighting design was by Frances Aronson; the sound design was by Bruce Ellman; and the production stage manager was Bess Marie Glorioso. The actor was Mark Setlock.

The Vineyard Theatre production of FULLY COMMITTED was subsequently presented Off-Broadway by David Stone, Jesse L. Martin, Adam Pascal and Susan Quint Gallin at The Cherry Lane Theatre (Angelina Fiordellisi, Executive Director; Joyce DiNicola-Friedman, Chief Financial Officer) in New York City.

AUTHOR'S NOTE: *Fully Committed* is a work of fiction. Any resemblance to actual persons living or dead is purely coincidental. While some of the characters bear the names of famous people, the portrayal of them in this play is entirely fictitious.

CHARACTERS

The performer will play forty different characters, including the reservationist, the chef, the maitre d', and all the various customers. Although *Fully Committed* was written with a male actor in mind, the role of SAM could easily be played by a woman.

SAM — a twenty-something out-of-work actor from the Midwest.

MRS. VANDEVERE — an old-moneyed Park Avenue socialite, on all the right social calendars and terminally dissatisfied. The modern equivalent of landed gentry.

THE SHEIK'S RIGHT-HAND MAN — completely humorless.

MRS. WINSLOW — the fine, upstanding wife of a Southern executive. Brimming with charm.

BRYCE — Naomi Campbell's personal assistant. Aggressively friendly and extremely effeminate, Bryce treats his work with the utmost gravity, as a neurosurgeon might.

MIDWESTERN SECRETARY — sensible and plainspoken.

CAROLANN ROSENSTEIN-FISHBURN — the ultimate restaurant regular. An iron-willed, nouveau-riche, helmet-haired socialite with far too much time on her hands.

STEPHANIE — the sweet-tempered British luncheon hostess.

OSCAR — the restaurant's fifty-two-year-old Lebanese business manager. Gentle, distracted, eccentric.

MRS. WATANABE — a painfully soft-spoken Japanese tourist. She understands very little English, but has learned a few words to help with making a reservation and the like.

BOB — more self-important and condescending than many a customer, he is the reservations manager. Afflicted with a loud, annoying laugh.

CHEF — Though he makes a big show of modesty, the Chef is a world-class narcissist, obsessively cultivating his own star status and worshipping at the altar of celebrity. Vain, petulant and mildly thuggish, the Chef seems more like an overgrown frat boy than the international culinary sensation that he is. He talks in an ultra-cool, disaffected, offhandedly sexy way, almost as if he's giving phone sex.

SAM'S DAD — a retired auto mechanic from the Midwest. Very sentimental when it comes to Sam, but not accustomed to expressing emotion.

JERRY MILLER — an old acting schoolmate of Sam's. An unctuous, competitive sycophant. (If the role of SAM is played by a woman, the role of JERRY should also be reconceived as female. Let's call her JENNY.)

JEAN-CLAUDE — the original French maitre d'. Wildly theatrical and drunk with his own power, he indiscriminately humiliates the various waiters, busboys and customers who cross him. Prone to frequent tantrums and intermittent bouts of charm, Jean-Claude can turn on a dime. One minute he's filled with contempt for the entire universe and the next he's maniacally fawning over a big tipper.

BELL ATLANTIC RECORDING WOMAN

SEXY RECORDED VOICE

CURTIS — Sam's agent's assistant. He has the aura of a queenie hairdresser — super bitchy, with a thick, almost Nuyorican accent. Loves to pontificate and has a soft spot for Sam.

DOMINICK VECCINI — a low-level mobster.

MRS. SEBAG (pronounced seabag) — always on the verge of total hysteria, waiting for the world to wrong her. She aggressively commandeers a large household staff, her husband Stanley, and anyone else who will let her.

HECTOR — a line cook from the Dominican Republic who does the chef's ordering and prepares the staff meal. Good at the requisite macho kitchen posturing, he is actually a closet softie.

MRS. BUXBAUM — a horrible combination of paranoid and aggressive, Mrs. Buxbaum is a reservationist's worst nightmare.

MR. DECOSTE — a mysterious stranger.

MR. ZAGAT

LARYNGITIS GUY — an incredibly nice guy who talks like he has laryngitis all the time.

JUDITH RUSH — a retired furniture dealer from a small town in upstate New York with delusions of grandeur and a constant sense that the world is cheating her. Still, sort of cute in spite of herself.

DEPRESSED SECRETARY — so miserable she barely has a pulse. Deeply resents her job.

PARAMOUNT LADY — a bitter workaholic.

STEVEN — Sam's perfect older brother. A real straight arrow.

GLORIA HATHAWAY — a food critic in the midst of a long-standing feud with the chef.

JEAN-CLAUDE'S WIFE — a big, tough French lady. Sounds a lot like Jean-Claude.

SMARMY MAN — a real smooth operator.

NANCY — Bob's girlfriend.

RICK FROM CARSON AVIATION — the kind of unflappable, even-keeled guy you want to have behind the controls of an airplane.

AT&T OPERATOR

MR. INOUE — a Japanese business executive.

DR. RUTH WESTHEIMER

PLACE

A dilapidated, windowless office in the basement of a four-star, multiple-award-winning, ridiculously trendy Upper East Side Manhattan restaurant. The ceiling seems as though it's about to cave in, and occasionally little pieces of insulation drift into what might be called the reservation department, which is actually a long, skinny Formica counter top and three folding chairs crammed into a four-foot by six-foot nook. The walls have been painted a particularly awful shade of industrial pale blue and plastered with little scraps of paper, some of which contain valuable information like the daily reservation counts, others of which issue ominous sounding warnings from the powers that be. One in particular, which seems to be extra large, reads: "Under no circumstances take a reservation for Ned Finlay: per chef!!!!" The office is scattered with telephones, fast-food paraphernalia, old newspapers, mounds of crumpled-up paper, staff coats and cartons of musty restaurant memorabilia. The business manager sits at a desk upstairs; the Chef's office is around the corner in a separate enclave.

TIME

Early December. There are a few pathetic signs of the Christmas season lying about: a candy cane here, a synthetic wreath there. More to the point, the phones are busier than ever.

NOTE: Text in **bold** should be pre-recorded.

FULLY COMMITTED

Lights up on the reservation office. The phones are ringing. Sam rushes down the stairs, puts on his headset and ...

(Sam — a twenty-something out-of-work actor from the Midwest.)

SAM. Good morning reservations; could you hold please?

(Mrs. Vandevere — an old-moneyed Park Avenue socialite, on all the right social calendars and terminally dissatisfied. The modern equivalent of landed gentry.)

MRS. VANDEVERE. Is the chef there?
SAM. No he's not. Could you hold please?
MRS. VANDEVERE. Is Jean-Claude there?
SAM. No he's not, could you hold please?
MRS. VANDEVERE. Is Bob there? *(The phone is still ringing.)*
SAM. No, he's not. Could you hold on for one second?
MRS. VANDEVERE. Ye-es.
SAM. Good morning, reservations, could you hold please?

(The Sheik's Right-Hand Man — completely humorless.)

SHEIK'S RIGHT-HAND MAN. I'm calling from Kuwait.
SAM. Okay, how can I help you? *(The phone is still ringing.)*
SHEIK'S RIGHT-HAND MAN. I'm calling to confirm dinner reservations for Sheik Akman Al Karafi tonight at nine-thirty.
SAM. Okay, I've got four at table thirty-one and two security

guards at table nineteen.

SHEIK'S RIGHT-HAND MAN. Yes, that's right. Thank you. *(The phone is still ringing.)*

SAM. *(On to a new line.)* Good morning, reservations; could you hold please?

(Mrs. Winslow — the fine, upstanding wife of a Southern executive. Brimming with charm.)

MRS. WINSLOW. Sure! *(The phone is still ringing.)*

SAM. *(On to a new line.)* Good morning, reservations; could you hold please?

(Bryce — Naomi Campbell's personal assistant. Aggressively friendly and extremely effeminate, Bryce treats his work with the utmost gravity, as a neurosurgeon might.)

BRYCE. Sure!

SAM. *(On to a new line.)* Good morning, reservations; could you hold please?

(Midwestern Secretary — sensible and plainspoken.)

MIDWESTERN SECRETARY. Sure!

SAM. *(On to a new line.)* Good morning, reservations; could you hold please? *(The phone stops ringing.)*

(Carolann Rosenstein-Fishburn — the ultimate restaurant regular. An iron-willed, nouveau-riche, helmet-haired socialite with far too much time on her hands.)

ROSENSTEIN-FISHBURN. Well I don't have a choice now do I? *(The phone rings again.)*

SAM. Good morning, reservations, could you hold please?

(Mrs. Watanabe — a painfully soft-spoken Japanese tourist. She understands very little English, but has learned a few words to help with making a reservation and the like.)

WATANABE. My name is Watanabe —
SAM. Could you hold please?
WATANABE. "W" as in Wisconsin. "A" as in —
SAM. One moment please. *(Sam buzzes upstairs.)* Bob? Hello upstairs. Sonya?

(Stephanie — the sweet-tempered British luncheon hostess.)

STEPHANIE. Morning Sam.
SAM. Hey Stephanie. Have you seen Bob? *(The phone rings.)*
STEPHANIE. No, but when he comes in will you tell him that there's a photographer from *Gourmet* magazine who's been waiting for the chef since eight-thirty. *(The phone is still ringing.)*
SAM. Okay. *(On to a new line.)* Reservations, could you hold please?
MRS. VANDEVERE. No, I tried that before. Who am I speaking with?
SAM. This is Sam.
MRS. VANDEVERE. *(Suddenly kissing up.)* Sam, darling, I didn't know you were still working there. It's Bunny Vandevere. *(A beat.)* My husband is Dick Vandevere.
SAM. Oh hi, how are you?
MRS. VANDEVERE. Well we're exhausted; we've just come back from Tibet. Now, I know it's last minute, but Mr. Vandevere and I want to come in tonight with our good friend Philip Johnson and we can be very flexible — anywhere between, say, seven-thirty and eight o'clock.
SAM. Okay, one moment please. *(Putting her on hold and buzzing upstairs.)* Hello upstairs. Jean-Claude? Oscar!! Oscar —

(Oscar — the restaurant's fifty-two-year-old Lebanese business manager. Gentle, distracted, eccentric.)

OSCAR. Sam, greetings and salutations. How are you?
SAM. Good, Oscar, how —
OSCAR. Did you see they had *The Grinch* on TV last night?
SAM. Yeah … hey, how V.I.P. is Mrs. Vandevere?
OSCAR. V.V.V.V.I.P.

SAM. She wants to come in tonight and I'm over by twenty-five.
OSCAR. Sam, her husband makes a lot of money. I think he invented Saran Wrap.
SAM. *(Back to Vandevere.)* Okay, Mrs. Vandevere. I just spoke to our business manager and you're all set for tonight. How about three people at seven-thirty? *(The phone rings.)*
MRS. VANDEVERE. That's marvelous, thank you so much Sam. And good luck to you!
SAM. *(On to a new line.)* Good morning, reservations, could you hold please?

(Bob — more self-important and condescending than many a customer, he is the reservations manager. Afflicted with a loud, annoying laugh.)

BOB. *(Mocking Sam.)* Good morning, reservations; could you hold please?
SAM. Hello?
BOB. *(Big laugh at his own joke.)* Hi Sam, it's Bob!
SAM. Hey Bob, where are you?
BOB. Not there!
SAM. Yeah, I know. Where are you?
BOB. The L.I.E.; can you believe it? My car stalled out in the middle of the passing lane.
SAM. No.
BOB. *(Melodramatic.)* I'm serious, Sam. I mean, it was the scariest thing that has *ever* happened to me. I mean, basically I'm lucky I'm still alive.
SAM. *(Unmoved.)* Well, when are you coming in?
BOB. *(Still cracking himself up.)* Don't go overboard with the sympathy, Sam. I'm waiting for a tow.
SAM. Where's Sonya?
BOB. Oh shit.
SAM. Shit what?
BOB. Sonya's not gonna be in today. *(Defensive.)* Look, she just found out her father has Lyme disease. And I didn't have time to cover her shift.
SAM. What?!
OSCAR. *(Buzzing in.)* Sam.

SAM. Yes, Oscar.

OSCAR. I'm going to the bank.

SAM. Okay.

BOB. Sam.

SAM. Yes, Bob.

BOB. I'll be there as soon as I can. You'll be fine! *(Another big laugh, then he hangs up.)*

SAM. *(Moving on to a new line.)* I'm sorry to keep you waiting, how can I help you?

MRS. WINSLOW. *(Syrupy sweet.)* I'm hoping you can! This is Mrs. Timothy Winslow calling from Louisville, Kentucky. My husband and I are coming to New York the weekend of January the thirteenth and we are just dyin' to come in and eat with y'all!

SAM. Ma'am, unfortunately we're fully committed that weekend.

MRS. WINSLOW. You're full of what now?

SAM. We're really, really, really full.

MRS. WINSLOW. But it's over a month away!

SAM. *(Apologetic.)* Actually, we work about two months in advance.

MRS. WINSLOW. Are you sure you don't have anything darlin'? We are two teeny tiny people.

SAM. Well, size isn't really the problem, ma'am. I just don't have anything at all weekends through February.

MRS. WINSLOW. *(Perky, even in defeat.)* Well darlin', I'm glad you people are doin' so well. Bye-bye! *(She hangs up.)*

SAM. *(New line.)* Thank you for holding, how can I help you?

BRYCE. *(Frighteningly cheerful.)* Hi, this is Bryce calling from Naomi Campbell's office!!!

SAM. Oh hi, Bryce. How are you?

BRYCE. I'm fine, thanks, who's this?!!!

SAM. Sam.

BRYCE. *(Pathologically excited to talk to Sam.)* Sam!!! I didn't know you were still working there! How are you?!!

SAM. Good, how are you?

BRYCE. Super! How's the acting career?

SAM. It's okay.

BRYCE. *(Gushing sympathy.)* Oh, it's such a tough business!! Hang in there!!

SAM. *(About to respond.)* Thanks I —

BRYCE. *(Not waiting for a reply; quickly shifting gears.)* Okay, Naomi would like to come in this weekend with fifteen people, on Saturday night at eight P.M., and she's gonna need a round, free-standing table, hold on for just one second ... *(Checking his records.)* ... it's number seventeen.

SAM. Okay.

BRYCE. Thanks! You can put that in her name. Naomi H. Campbell. And you can confirm that with me. I'm Bryce!!

SAM. Right, and the number there?

BRYCE. *(Very hush-hush.)* Okay, it's 866-2250 and I know you'll be discreet with that information.

SAM. Of course.

BRYCE. Thanks! And you know she doesn't eat dairy, right?

SAM. Right.

BRYCE. And no female waitstaff at the table!

SAM. Okay.

BRYCE. Thanks a million!

SAM. *(On to another line.)* Thank you for holding, how can I help you?

MIDWESTERN SECRETARY. Good morning, I'm phoning from the offices of Dr. Frank Mallone up here in Milwaukee. He's planning a trip to New York later this month and he'd like some details regarding your cuisine.

SAM. All right, the chef calls it "global fusion."

MIDWESTERN SECRETARY. *(Stymied.)* Okay, could you fax us over a menu?

SAM. *(Grabbing an old menu.)* Well, the chef changes the menu from day to day, but I could read you a few items off last night's menu, if you'd like.

MIDWESTERN SECRETARY. That'd be great.

SAM. *(Reeling it off, matter-of-fact.)* All right, we've got jicama-smoked Scottish wood squab poached in a ginger broth and wrapped in wilted spinach.

MIDWESTERN SECRETARY. *(Dumbfounded.)* Okay ...

SAM. And herb-crusted grouper speckled with fresh hyssop oil on a bed of wild ramps.

MIDWESTERN SECRETARY. *(Still dumbfounded.)* Okay ...

SAM. And Argentinian cedar roasted milk-fed organic chicken.

MIDWESTERN SECRETARY. *(At last a familiar item.)* Oh, good you do have chicken and things of that nature, okay! And what is the average price of a meal?

SAM. Somewhere between one hundred and two hundred dollars a head, depending on —

MIDWESTERN SECRETARY. *(A little more than she'd bargained for.)* Okay then, thanks for your help! *(She hangs up.)*

SAM. *(On to a new line.)* Thank you for holding, how can I help you?

ROSENSTEIN-FISHBURN. *(Like a drill sergeant.)* First of all, I've been holding for ten minutes! Number two, you have to do something about that music. Those crescendos are really very piercing. All right now, I need to speak to Jean-Claude regarding Friday evening. It's Carolann Rosenstein-Fishburn.

SAM. He's not in yet, can I — *(Dial tone; she's hung up.)* Hello? *(The phone rings. Sam moves on to the new line.)* Good morning, reservations, could you hold please?

(Chef — Though he makes a big show of modesty, the Chef is a world-class narcissist, obsessively cultivating his own star status and worshipping at the altar of celebrity. Vain, petulant and mildly thuggish, the Chef seems more like an overgrown frat boy than the international culinary sensation that he is. He talks in an ultra-cool, disaffected, offhandedly sexy way, almost as if he's giving phone sex.)

CHEF. *(Barely awake, he's calling from bed.)* Who's this?

SAM. Hi Chef, it's Sam.

CHEF. Sam, how's it going?

SAM. Good, I —

CHEF. Lemme talk to Jean-Claude.

SAM. He's not here yet —

CHEF. Lemme talk to Oscar.

SAM. He just went to the ba —

CHEF. Lemme talk to Bob.

SAM. *(Anticipating a hissy fit.)* He's not —

CHEF. *(Having a hissy fit.)* What the fuck is going on over there?!! Where's Bob?

SAM. His car just broke down on the L.I.E.

CHEF. So who's on the phones?

SAM. Just me right now.

CHEF. *(Snarling.)* Just you? Where's Sonya?

SAM. She just found out her father has Lyme disease.

CHEF. *(Deeply paranoid.)* Yeah? That's a good one. Tell her I need a doctor's note.

SAM. Okay.

CHEF. Pass me up to the hostess. *(The phone rings.)*

SAM. *(Buzzing upstairs.)* Stephanie, Chef on line two. *(On to his new line.)* Reservations, could you hold please?

(Sam's Dad — a retired auto mechanic from the Midwest. Very sentimental when it comes to Sam, but not accustomed to expressing emotion.)

DAD. I dunno, Sammo!

SAM. Hey Dad, how are you doing?

DAD. Oh not too bad. How 'bout you?

SAM. Pretty good.

DAD. How'd ya do on that play audition?

SAM. Oh pretty good.

DAD. Didja get the article I sent you on the guy from *Ally McBeal*?

SAM. Yeah, thanks.

DAD. You know he graduated St. Bridget's about three years after you left. *(The phone rings.)*

SAM. Really?

DAD. I didn't even know he was an actor. *(The phone rings again.)*

SAM. Dad, can you hold on for one second?

DAD. Okey-doke.

SAM. *(New line.)* Reservations, could you hold please?

(Jerry Miller — an old acting schoolmate of Sam's. An unctuous, competitive sycophant.)

JERRY. Hey babe, it's Jerry.

SAM. Hey Jerry, could you hold on for one second?

JERRY. *(Ingratiating.)* Take your time.

SAM. *(Back to Dad.)* Sorry Dad. *(The phone rings again.)*

DAD. That's okay.

SAM. I'm sorry, can you hold on for one more second?

DAD. Okey-doke.

SAM. *(On to the new line.)* Reservations, could you hold please?

BRYCE. Yeah, it's Bryce; I'll hold!!

SAM. *(Back to Dad.)* Dad, you know what? I should probably try and get through these lines.

DAD. Okay kiddo; hey — didja ask the chef about Christmas?

SAM. He still hasn't made up his mind.

DAD. You know today's the last day for that twenty-one day advance deal on US AIR.

SAM. Yeah I know.

STEPHANIE. *(Buzzing in.)* Sam! It's the chef on line two.

SAM. Dad, let me call you back in one minute. That's the chef.

DAD. Okey-doke. Adios amigo. *(He hangs up.)*

SAM. *(On to line two.)* Chef?

CHEF. *(Still half asleep.)* What did we do last night?

SAM. *(Checking a list.)* It looks like $22,700.

CHEF. What does lunch look like?

SAM. We're all booked up.

CHEF. *(Snarling.)* What did you just say?

SAM. I'm sorry, we're —

CHEF. Did you forget my new policy?

SAM. No, we're "fully committed."

CHEF. That's more like it. Any V.I.P.s?

SAM. *(Reading off another list.)* Yeah, there's Diane Sawyer at twelve.

CHEF. Who's that?

SAM. She's a famous TV reporter.

CHEF. *(Unimpressed.)* Oh. Anyone else?

SAM. Henry Kravis at two-thirty.

CHEF. Who's that?

SAM. I don't know. The name sounds familiar but I don't really know who he is.

CHEF. *(Losing interest.)* Yeah, who gives a shit. *(He hangs up.)*

SAM. *(On to his waiting lines.)* Thank you for holding, how can I help you?

WATANABE. My name is Watanabe. "W" as in Wisconsin, "A" as —

SAM. *(Very patient.)* Okay. How can I help you?

WATANABE. *(Delicate, cautious.)* I want to take a table.

SAM. Okay, when would you like to come in?

WATANABE. We are four people.

SAM. All right. When would you like to come in?

WATANABE. Four people.

SAM. Okay … What day of the week would you like to come in?

WATANABE. Four.

SAM. I'll be right with you ma'am. *(Puts her on hold, takes a deep breath, then returns.)* Sorry about that.

WATANABE. No have four?

SAM. No, no. *(Trying a new tactic.)* Four people on Monday? Tuesday? Wednesday?

WATANABE. Ohhh! Tuesday.

SAM. Okay, Tuesday. Would you like to come in for lunch or dinner?

WATANABE. *(Getting it.)* Lunch!

SAM. Okay! Lunch on Tuesday. What time?

WATANABE. Seven P.M.

SAM. Ma'am. That's dinner.

WATANABE. Dinner?

SAM. Yes seven P.M. is dinner and we are fully committed for dinner on Tuesday.

WATANABE. Ful-ly?

SAM. We don't have any tables.

WATANABE. Oh, I call you back. *(She hangs up.)*

SAM. *(On to a new line.)* Thank you for holding, how can I help you?

JERRY. Sam, it's Jerry …

SAM. I'm sorry, Jerry. I forgot you were there.

JERRY. God, I don't know how you do it, Sam. If I had your job, I'd shoot myself. *(And then.)* So … how was your callback?!

SAM. It was okay; how was yours?

JERRY. Really really good. I'm going in for a final callback this afternoon.

SAM. *(Taken aback.)* Really.

JERRY. *(Playing sensitive.)* Oh God, I knew I shouldn't have said anything. Is this weird for you?
SAM. No it's fine, congratulations.
JERRY. I mean, they could still call you back, Sam. I mean you're so fucking good.
SAM. Thanks Jerry.
JERRY. I still can't believe that HBO thing fell through. I mean, you were perfect for the part.
SAM. Thanks.
JERRY. Look Sam, I know it's hard sometimes, but I just feel like we need to be really honest with each other about this whole audition process.
SAM. Yeah, me too —
JERRY. *(Checking his caller I.D.)* Oo, that's my other line. Let me call you right back. *(He hangs up. The phone rings.)*
SAM. Reservations, could you hold please?
ROSENSTEIN-FISHBURN. It's Carolann Rosenstein-Fishburn calling for Jean-Claude. Did you forget to give him the message?
SAM. One moment please. *(Buzzing upstairs.)* Hello upstairs! Jean-Claude!

(Jean-Claude — the original French maitre d'. Wildly theatrical and drunk with his own power, he indiscriminately humiliates the various waiters, busboys and customers who cross him. Prone to frequent tantrums and intermittent bouts of charm, Jean-Claude can turn on a dime. One minute he's filled with contempt for the entire universe and the next he's maniacally fawning over a big tipper.)

JEAN-CLAUDE. Allo, be brief.
SAM. Hi Jean-Claude, it's Sam.
JEAN-CLAUDE. *(Mildly pleased that it's Sam.)* Sam, what can I do for you? *(And then snippy.)* I'm trying to get ready for lunch up here!!
SAM. Carolann Rosenstein-Fishburn on line four.
JEAN-CLAUDE. *(Disgusted.)* Oh my God, I hate that lady. No sex appeal at all.
SAM. Do you want to talk to her?
JEAN-CLAUDE. She's so ugly Sam, you can't believe it. She has

a face like a dog.

SAM. Jean-Claude.

JEAN-CLAUDE. I'm just telling you the fact of the situation.

SAM. *(Back to Mrs. Fishburn.)* Okay Mrs. Fishburn, I can't find Jean-Claude, but I'll have him call you as soon as he gets in.

ROSENSTEIN-FISHBURN. Who is this?

SAM. Sam.

ROSENSTEIN-FISHBURN. Sam, tell Jean-Claude it's an urgent situation.

SAM. Are you sure there's nothing I — *(Dial tone; she's hung up. Sam moves on to a new line.)* Thank you for holding, how can I help you?

BRYCE. Hi Sam, it's Bryce from Naomi Campbell's office!!!

SAM. Hi Bryce, what can I do for you?

BRYCE. Listen, I can't remember if I specified that Naomi wants an all-vegan tasting menu on Saturday night, did I?

SAM. No, actually you didn't.

BRYCE. Oh sweet Mary! That's why I always double check these things three and four times!!! Okay, so she definitely needs an all-vegan tasting menu. That's a no-fat, no-salt, no-dairy, no-sugar, no-chicken, no-meat, no-fish, no-soy tasting menu for fifteen, okay?

SAM. Okay, I'll make a note of that.

BRYCE. Super, thanks a trillion!! *(He hangs up. A beat — Sam is listening for something … silence. He calls his answering machine.)*

MACHINE/SAM'S VOICE. **Hi, you've reached 522-7003. Please leave a message for Sam.** *(Sam punches in the code.)*

MACHINE VOICE. **Hello. You have one message.**

(Bell Atlantic Recording Voice.)

BELL ATLANTIC RECORDING VOICE. *(Computer-generated sound.)* **This is** … *(A big, deep booming voice, sounds something like James Earl Jones.)* **Bell Atlantic** … *(Back to computer-generated voice.)* **calling with a message for** … *(Bad Brooklyn accent.)* **Sam Peliczowski.** *(Back to computer-generated voice.)* **It is important that you call our business offices before five P.M. today or call our automated payment line at 869-9000.**

ANSWERING MACHINE VOICE. **That was your last message.**
(Still no phones. Sam discreetly dials another number.)

(Sexy Recorded Voice.)

SEXY RECORDED VOICE. **You have reached** *The Village Voice*
**Personals Network. The cost of this call is $1.95 per minute and
you must be eighteen years or older to use this service. Please
enter your four digit password now.** *(Sam enters the code.)* **You
have no messages.** *(Still no phones. Sam makes one last call.)*

*(Curtis — Sam's agent's assistant. He has the aura of a queenie hair-
dresser — super bitchy — with a thick, almost Nuyorican accent.
Loves to pontificate and has a soft spot for Sam.)*

CURTIS. Diana Drake Agency.
SAM. Hi Curtis, it's Sam.
CURTIS. *(Tired.)* Sam, how are you?
SAM. Pretty good, could I talk to Diana?
CURTIS. She's ... *(Silently communicating with Diana, who's dodg-
ing Sam.)* ... in a meeting, is there something I can help you with?
SAM. I was just calling to see if you had heard anything from
Lincoln Center.
CURTIS. Sam, if we would had heard anything I would have
called you.
SAM. No, it's just that I was talking to Jerry Miller and he said
he's going back in this afternoon and —
CURTIS. Sam, why don't you worry about your career and let
Jerry worry about Jerry's.
SAM. No, I just wanted to know if today was the last day they're
seeing people.
CURTIS. I have no idea. *(The phone starts to ring.)*
SAM. Well, can you have Diana call me when she gets back? I'm
at the restaurant.
CURTIS. *(Unimpressed.)* Oh ... I didn't know you were still
working there.
SAM. Yeah, I'm still working here. *(It's still ringing.)*
CURTIS. All right Sam, I'll give her the message. Ciao.

SAM. *(Finally picking up the phone.)* Reservations, could you hold please?

CHEF. Sam, how many times is the phone supposed to ring before you pick it up?

SAM. *(Sheepish.)* Two.

CHEF. And how many times was that?

SAM. Sorry, Chef.

CHEF. I'm in the cab. Any messages?

SAM. *(Reading from a message pad.)* Yeah, there are a few from last night. Jamie Lee Curtis called.

CHEF. *(Perking up.)* Really? She's so hot. Anyone else?

SAM. Your yoga instructor called; there's a message from your Ferrari dealer and something from your mother.

CHEF. Really? What does the Ferrari dealer want?

SAM. He wanted to let you know that he's FedExing your global positioning unit.

CHEF. *(Like a little kid.)* Oh cool!! All right, I'll be there in five. *(He hangs up. The phone rings.)*

SAM. Reservations, could you hold please?

(Dominick Veccini — a low-level mobster.)

VECCINI. All right.

SAM. *(Buzzing upstairs.)* Steph — is the staff meal up?

STEPHANIE. Give me two seconds. I've just got to seat my twelve-fifteen. *(The phone rings.)*

SAM. Reservations, could you hold please?

(Mrs. Sebag (pronounced seabag) — always on the verge of total hysteria, waiting for the world to wrong her. She aggressively commandeers a large household staff, her husband Stanley and anyone else who will let her.)

SEBAG. *(Livid.)* No I cannot!

SAM. *(Getting testy.)* Okay, how can I help you?

SEBAG. *(To an offstage lackey.)* No, Maria, don't put it there. You're going to scratch the floors — *(To Sam.)* I'm calling to confirm my reservation for Saturday night.

SAM. And your name?

SEBAG. Sebag. S-E-B-A-G.

SAM. And how many people?

SEBAG. Three.

SAM. And what time?

SEBAG. Six or six thirty. I don't know. *(To Maria.)* No Maria, I'll be right there! *(To Sam, trying to get off the phone.)* All right, am I set?

SAM. I don't see it here ma'am, could it be under another name?

SEBAG. *(Starting to flip.)* What do you — No, it's under Sebag.

SAM. Well, I'm looking under Sebag right now and I don't see it anywhere so I'm wondering if there's another name you could have put it under.

SEBAG. *(Gearing up for battle.)* Do you mean to tell me — I made it myself under the name of Sebag! What's going on there?

SAM. Well ma'am, I —

SEBAG. *(Her fury is peaking.)* Oh my — I cannot believe this is happening!! *(Screaming, to offstage husband.)* Stanley, they don't have our reservation!! Oh my God!

SAM. Ma'am —

SEBAG. *(Moving into the grief phase.)* I can't believe you're doing this to me!! *(The phone rings.)*

SAM. Okay ma'am, could you hold for just a second?

SEBAG. No!

SAM. Ma'am, I have to get this phone, I'll be right back. *(On to his new line.)* Reservations, can you hold please?

MRS. VANDEVERE. Sam, it's Bunny Vandevere!

SAM. I'll be right with you. *(Back to Sebag.)* Okay ma'am, I'm —

SEBAG. Who am I speaking to?

SAM. *(Beat, a strategic decision.)* Herbert.

SEBAG. Herbert, put me on with a manager!!

SAM. Ma'am, right now the reservation manager isn't here, but I can take a message and he'll call you back.

SEBAG. No, Herbert! This is an emergency.

SAM. *(Trying logic.)* Okay then, what I'd like to do first is read all the parties of three I have on Saturday in case the reservation was mistakenly put at the wrong time or under the wrong name, okay?

SEBAG. *(Left with no alternative.)* Ach — all right go ahead!!

SAM. Okay: Duff. Lamb. Tisch.

SEBAG. No-no-no.

SAM. Buckley. Burden. Peyton. Miller.

SEBAG. No-no-no-no.

SAM. And Yamaguchi.

SEBAG. *(Shrieking.)* No!!!

SAM. I'm sorry, ma'am … I don't know what else to tell you right now. I —

MRS. SEBAG. Tell me that you'll honor my reservation which I made over three months ago!!

SAM. I can't do that until our reservation manager gets —

SEBAG. *(Howling.)* Stanley! *(She hangs up.)*

SAM. *(Back to his other line.)* I'm so sorry, sir, how can I help you?

VECCINI. Yeah, my parents are regulars with youse and they're coming in tonight at five for their anniversary. And I wanted to see if the waiters could sing their favorite song at the table.

SAM. *(Taking the information down.)* Okay, what's the name of the song?

VECCINI. *(Trying to keep his cool.)* "The Lady is a Tramp."

SAM. *(Amused.)* And their names?

VECCINI. Veccini.

SAM. Okay hold on. *(Buzzing upstairs.)* Jean-Claude?

JEAN-CLAUDE. Ye-ees.

SAM. There's a guy on line three who wants one of the waiters to sing "The Lady is a Tramp" for his parents' anniversary tonight.

JEAN-CLAUDE. Oh my God! That's so tacky!

SAM. What do you want to do?

JEAN-CLAUDE. *(Disgusted by the mere thought.)* What's the name?

SAM. Veccini.

JEAN-CLAUDE. *(Apparently he's a good tipper.)* Oh my God, are you kidding?! Of course!! Give him whatever he wants! The guy's a Mafia.

SAM. How much are you going to charge him?

JEAN-CLAUDE. I don't know … one — no … two-hundred and ninety-five dollars.

SAM. Well pick up line three. *(On to a new line.)* Thank you for holding, how can I help you?

MRS. VANDEVERE. *(Needling.)* Sam, it's Bunny Vandevere. You must be awfully busy today!

SAM. Yeah we —

MRS. VANDEVERE. Listen, I forgot to tell you, we're going to need table thirty-one tonight.

SAM. *(Looking for his dinner list.)* That shouldn't be a — *(Finding it.)* Actually someone's reserved table thirty-one tonight.

MRS. VANDEVERE. *(Unfazed.)* Well, we always sit there; we sort of have a standing reservation.

SAM. Well, actually we have a lot of customers who like to sit there and it's been reserved.

MRS. VANDEVERE. Sam, we're coming in with Philip Johnson, you do you know who he is, don't you?

SAM. Yes I —

MRS. VANDEVERE. He's the most important living architect in this country.

SAM. No I just — the table's been reserved.

MRS. VANDEVERE. Well, who reserved it?

SAM. I can't tell you that, Mrs. Vandevere.

MRS. VANDEVERE. Why not? I'm going to see who's sitting there anyway. *(A beat.)* Is it Carolann Rosenstein-Fishburn?

SAM. *(Reluctantly.)* No, his name is Sheik Akman Al Karafi, okay?

MRS. VANDEVERE. Well, why don't you give us table nineteen then.

SAM. That's actually been reserved too.

MRS. VANDEVERE. *(Deeply peeved.)* Oh for heaven's sake, Sam, it's not rocket science. Why don't you have Bob call me when he gets in? You don't seem to be have the authority to handle it by yourself. *(She hangs up. The Chef's special phone buzzes, indicating that he's in his office. From this point on, each time Sam has to communicate with the Chef, he has to get up and use this special "bat" phone.)*

SAM. Yes, Chef?

CHEF. I'm in my office. Let me talk to Bob.

SAM. He's still not here.

CHEF. That's great. Any new messages?

SAM. No.

CHEF. Did Mickey Rourke call?

SAM. No.

CHEF. *(Pissy.)* Damn it. *(Impetuous.)* All right from now on, I have another new policy. I want you to transfer every single one of my calls straight to my office. I'm sick of you guys deciding who I get to talk to, okay? That's my privilege.

SAM. Of course.

CHEF. But if Ned Finlay calls, you can tell him that I don't ever want to see his fat ass in this restaurant again, all right?

SAM. Okay.

CHEF. And don't forget about my helicopter. *(The phone starts ringing.)*

SAM. I'm sorry? *(Still ringing.)*

CHEF. I need a helicopter to the airport tonight. My flight's at seven. *(And more ringing.)*

SAM. Okay. *(Finally picking up.)* Reservations, how can I help you?

SEBAG. *(Still in a state, to Stanley.)* They are not answering the — hello? *(To Sam.)* Herbert, put me on with the chef right now! It's Mrs. Sebag.

SAM. One moment please. *(Sam heads to the bat phone.)* Chef.

CHEF. Ye-es?

SAM. *(Mischievous, knowing full well that the Chef does not want to talk to Mrs. Sebag.)* Line two for you. *(Buzzing upstairs.)* Stephanie! Is the food up?

STEPHANIE. Sorry, I'll go and check right now. *(The Chef buzzes in. Sam runs back to the bat phone.)*

SAM. Yes, Chef?

CHEF. Who the hell is Mrs. Sebag?

SAM. She's a customer who's upset be —

CHEF. Sam, use your brain. I didn't mean transfer EVERY goddamn call. *(He hangs up.)*

SAM. *(Back to Sebag.)* Okay Mrs. Sebag, the chef's been detained, but the minute Bob gets in I'll have him call you, okay? *(The phone rings.)*

SEBAG. *(Still enraged.)* This is UNBELIEVABLE! *(She hangs up.)*

SAM. *(On to a new line.)* Reservations, could you hold please?

DAD. Hey-a kiddo, didja forget about your old man?

SAM. Oh hey, dad. I'm sorry.

DAD. That's okay kiddo. Didja ask the chef about Christmas yet?

SAM. Yeah … let me ask him right now and call you back.

DAD. Okey-doke. Adios. *(He hangs up. Sam heads to the bat*

phone.)

SAM. Chef?

CHEF. *(Annoyed.)* What do you want?

SAM. I was wondering if you decided whether we're open on Christmas or not?

CHEF. Open.

SAM. And Christmas Eve?

CHEF. Open.

SAM. And are you gonna need me and Bob?

CHEF. Well, I need one of you and if I'm not mistaken, Bob has seniority.

SAM. Okay, thanks. *(Sam starts to dial his dad's number, but can't go through with it.)*

STEPHANIE. *(Buzzing in.)* Sam, you're not going to like this.

SAM. What?

STEPHANIE. The staff meal's gone; they put it out without buzzing us.

SAM. No.

STEPHANIE. I'm sorry, love. I think Bob's got some Cheetos in his file cabinet.

SAM. Thanks. *(Buzzing up to the kitchen, which is really loud.)* Hello? Hello in the kitchen! Hector?

(Hector — a line cook from the Dominican Republic who does the Chef's ordering and prepares the staff meal. Good at the requisite macho kitchen posturing, he is actually a closet softie.)

HECTOR. Yeah what's up, Papi? We busy.

SAM. Sorry, I just wanted to know if you ever made the staff meal?

HECTOR. What do you mean did I ever make it?

SAM. Well, I never got any.

HECTOR. That's not my problem, Papi, I made it.

SAM. Well, no one told me it was up so I never got any.

HECTOR. That's different, okay? If you didn't know is up is different. Because I made it okay?

SAM. *(Getting testy.)* Okay, but I can't leave the office today so I never knew you made it. *(The phone rings.)*

HECTOR. So what do you want me to do, Papi? Why you get-

29

ting your attitude at me? *(Still ringing.)*

SAM. *(To Hector.)* I'm not, I'm just really hungry. Never mind. *(On to a new line.)* Reservations, could you hold please?

(A horrible combination of paranoid and aggressive — Mrs. Buxbaum is a reservationist's worst nightmare.)

BUXBAUM. *(Grotesquely angry.)* No, this is Mrs. Buxbaum! It is vital that I speak to the chef ASAP!

SAM. He's in a meeting right now, can I ask what it's in regard to?

BUXBAUM. Yes, I was speaking with a Sam earlier this morning and he was extremely rude.

SAM. *(Taken aback.)* This is Sam.

BUXBAUM. Well I don't know who you thought you were speaking to this morning, but I will not stand for it!

SAM. *(Genuinely confused.)* I'm sorry ma'am, did we speak this morning?

BUXBAUM. What do you mean, did we speak this morning?!! Are you accusing me of lying?!!!

SAM. No I just — *(And suddenly Mrs. Buxbaum bursts into hysterical laughter, revealing herself to be Bob, playing a practical joke.)*

BOB. Hi Sam, it's Bob! You didn't know who I was did you?

SAM. Yeah, you're hilarious. Where are you?

BOB. I told you Sam; I'm waiting for a tow.

SAM. Oh my — Bob, it's one-thirty and I haven't even eaten yet.

BOB. Sam, what do you want me to tell you?

SAM. I just want you to hurry up and get here.

BOB. Lighten up, champ. I'm doin' the best I can.

SAM. Well, hurry.

STEPHANIE. *(Buzzing in.)* Sam!

SAM. *(To Stephanie.)* Yes?

STEPHANIE. *(Furtive.)* Do you know anything about … Mr. Zagat coming in today?

SAM. *(Understanding the magnitude of the situation.)* No.

STEPHANIE. Well, he's up here and he's not on the list.

SAM. *(Complete disbelief.)* No.

STEPHANIE. Yes.

SAM. *(Rifling through his lists, panicking.)* Well, I don't see anything about it down here.

STEPHANIE. He insists he made a reservation last week.

SAM. Can you bump somebody?

STEPHANIE. I've just sat my last table. *(Beat; as if she's announcing a major tragedy.)* I think he's going to have to wait.

SAM. *(A disaster of epic proportions.)* Oh my God.

STEPHANIE. Where's the chef?

SAM. In his office.

STEPHANIE. Buzz me if he comes up this way. *(The bat phone buzzes. Sam rushes over and picks it up.)*

SAM. Yes, Chef?

CHEF. I'm going upstairs.

SAM. Okay. *(Buzzing Stephanie.)* Steph!! He's on his way upstairs.

STEPHANIE. Oh God.

JEAN-CLAUDE. *(Buzzing in, seething.)* Allo, Sam!! What is going on down there? I have Mr. and Mrs. Zagat waiting in the lounge for a table!

SAM. *(Floundering.)* I don't know. They weren't on the list.

JEAN-CLAUDE. *(Foaming at the mouth.)* I know they not on the list, otherwise I would have known they were coming and I would have had their table ready for them.

SAM. I'm sorry; I didn't talk to him. Maybe Bob spoke to —

JEAN-CLAUDE. Well, put Bob on the phone.

SAM. He's not here.

JEAN-CLAUDE. *(Losing his mind.)* Ohhhhh this is wonderful! Now Mr. and Mrs. Zagat going to have to wait twenty, maybe thirty minutes because I got Mr. Hiashi at table one and forty-five people waiting for tables in the lounge!!!! *(He hangs up.)*

OSCAR. *(Buzzing in.)* Sam.

SAM. Yes, Oscar?

OSCAR. *(A beat.)* I forgot what I was going to say.

SAM. *(Patient.)* Well, buzz me back if you remember. *(The Chef buzzes in. Sam runs to the bat phone.)*

SAM. Yes, Chef?

CHEF. What the hell's going on down there?

SAM. *(Guilt-ridden.)* Nothing.

CHEF. What is Tim Zagat doing in the lounge?

SAM. I don't know, there's nothing down here about it.

CHEF. What do you mean there's nothing down there about it? What are you doing all fucking day?

SAM. I mean, I never spoke to him and there's no note or —

CHEF. Get Zagat on the line. *(The phone rings.)*

SAM. What? *(The phone is still ringing.)*

CHEF. I want you to buzz up to the lounge and ask Zagat who he talked to.

SAM. Okay. *(On to his new line, flustered.)* Good morning — good afternoon, reservations, could you hold please?

(Mr. Decoste — a mysterious stranger.)

MR. DECOSTE. I'd like to come in tonight at seven-thirty.

SAM. *(Distracted.)* Unfortunately sir, we're fully committed tonight.

MR. DECOSTE. So what'll it cost me?

SAM. What'll it cost you?

MR. DECOSTE. I'm assuming that for the right price, you could find me a table.

SAM. *(Dawning on him.)* Oh … actually sir, we're not supposed to accept any kind of —

MR. DECOSTE. *(Amused.)* All right, what's your name?

SAM. Sam.

MR. DECOSTE. All right, thank you, Sam. *(He hangs up. The Chef buzzes in. Sam runs to the bat phone.)*

SAM. Yes, Chef?

CHEF. What did Zagat say?

SAM. I haven't —

CHEF. *(Barking.)* Now!!

SAM. Okay. *(Buzzing upstairs.)* Steph? Can you put Zagat on the line?

STEPHANIE. Mr. Zagat?

SAM. Don't even ask.

STEPHANIE. *(Confused, handing the phone to Mr. Zagat.)* All right.

(Mr. Zagat.)

ZAGAT. Tim Zagat.

SAM. Hi, Mr. Zagat, this is Sam from downstairs … the chef actually wanted me to ask you who you spoke to last week when you made the reservation.

ZAGAT. *(Miffed.)* My assistant called and confirmed this twice.

SAM. Yeah, actually we're just trying to correct the situation down here. Do you remember who you spoke to?

ZAGAT. It was Bob. I always speak to Bob. *(The phone starts to ring.)*

SAM. *(Cheered.)* Okay, thank you so much! *(Picking up his new line.)* Good afternoon, reservations; could you hold please?

(Laryngitis Guy — an incredibly nice guy who talks like he has laryngitis all the time.)

LARYNGITIS GUY. Absolutely! *(The Chef buzzes. Sam runs to the bat phone.)*

SAM. Yes, Chef?

CHEF. Who did Zagat speak with?

SAM. *(Joyous.)* Bob.

CHEF. I'm gonna cut his fucking balls off. *(He hangs up.)*

SAM. *(Gleefully moving on to a new line.)* Thank you for holding, how can I help you?

LARYNGITIS GUY. *(Genuine, pleasant.)* You're very welcome. Who'm I speaking with?

SAM. *(Taken aback by the sound of his voice.)* Sam.

LARYNGITIS GUY. Sam, how are you today?

SAM. I'm good; sounds like you have a bad cold.

LARYNGITIS GUY. No, this is how I talk. It's sort of a permanent cold.

SAM. Oh, is it sort of like nodes?

LARYNGITIS GUY. No, I was just born this way.

SAM. Well, do you do any exercises for it — like vocal warm-ups? *(The phone rings.)*

LARYNGITIS GUY. No, what do you mean?

SAM. Hold on one second. *(New line.)* Reservations, could you hold please?

(Depressed Secretary — so miserable, she barely has a pulse. Deeply

resents her job.)

DEPRESSED SECRETARY. I guess so.
SAM. *(Back to Laryngitis Guy.)* Yeah, I had this old acting teacher who used to make us do this whole routine to make sure we didn't strain our vocal chords. You should try it.
LARYNGITIS GUY. What do I do?
SAM. Just try opening your mouth as wide as you can, like you were about to yawn and say — *(Opening his mouth and talking like an idiot.)* Hello.
LARYNGITIS GUY. *(His version sounds like a retarded person with laryngitis.)* Hello. *(The phone rings.)*
SAM. Great. Hold on one second okay?
LARYNGITIS GUY. *(Still sounding bizarre.)* Okay!
SAM. *(On to his new line.)* Reservations, could you hold please?

(Judith Rush — a retired furniture dealer from a small town in upstate New York with delusions of grandeur and a constant sense that the world is cheating her. Still, sort of cute in spite of herself.)

JUDITH RUSH. Hello? Hell — *(The phone is still ringing.)*
SAM. I'll be right with you, ma'am. *(New line.)* Reservations, could you hold please?
BRYCE. Yeah, it's Bryce, I'll hold!
SAM. *(Back to Laryngitis Guy.)* Sir?
LARYNGITIS GUY. *(Still talking funny.)* Yeah.
SAM. Why don't you give me your name and number and I'll call you back as soon as I get rid of these lines, okay?
LARYNGITIS GUY. My name's Dan Rappaport and our number here is 219-223-9008.
SAM. That's South Bend.
LARYNGITIS GUY. It sure is.
SAM. That's where I grew up.
LARYNGITIS GUY. No sir. What's your last name, Sam?
SAM. Peliczowski.
LARYNGITIS GUY. As in Peliczowski Auto Body?
SAM. That's my dad.
LARYNGITIS GUY. I've known your dad for twenty-five years.

SAM. No way.

LARYNGITIS GUY. Oh sure. You're Sam, the actor in New York — right?

SAM. Yeah …

LARYNGITIS GUY. *(And then.)* Hey listen, I was real sorry to hear about your mom.

SAM. Oh, thanks.

LARYNGITIS GUY. How's your dad doing?

SAM. He's doing all right.

LARYNGITIS GUY. You guys taking good care of him?

SAM. Yeah. *(The Chef buzzes in.)* Hold on for just one second, Mr. Rappaport. *(Sam runs to the bat phone.)* Yes, Chef?

CHEF. Pull the Zagat file.

SAM. Okay, hold on one second. *(Sam runs back to the phones. The Chef keeps buzzing. Sam picks up the phone.)* Mr. Rappaport, I've got to do something for my boss. Let me call you back when it calms down, okay? *(More buzzing.)*

LARYNGITIS GUY. Okay Sam; you take care now. *(He hangs up. Sam gets the Zagat file and runs back to the bat phone.)*

SAM. Chef, I —

CHEF. What appetizers did he eat the last time he was here?

SAM. *(Reading from the file.)* It looks like marinated fluke, grilled quail salad and terrine of head cheese.

CHEF. Did he finish all his dishes?

SAM. Looks like everything except the terrine —

CHEF. *(Seething.)* Motherfuck! Buzz Jean-Claude and tell him to hold the head cheese.

SAM. Okay. *(Buzzing Jean-Claude.)* Jean-Claude. Chef wants you to hold Zagat's head cheese.

JEAN-CLAUDE. Tell the chef to hold his own head cheese. *(He hangs up.)*

SAM. *(On to a new line.)* Thank you for holding, how can I help you?

DEPRESSED SECRETARY. I've been holding so long I forgot who I called.

SAM. This is Restaur —

DEPRESSED SECRETARY. Oh right, you guys. Who else would keep me on hold for that long? Okay, I'm calling for Gloria

Hathaway from *Gourmet* magazine. She wants to talk to the chef.

SAM. One moment please. *(Sam heads to the bat phone.)* Chef?

CHEF. What the fuck do you want?!

SAM. Gloria Hathaway's secretary is on line three.

CHEF. Tell her I'm not here.

SAM. You do know about the photographer from *Gourmet* magazine waiting in the lounge?

CHEF. *(Mocking Sam.)* Sam, you do know that I'm trying to prepare an alternate appetizer for the Zagats, who've also been waiting in our lounge for over twenty fucking minutes like regular fucking customers. *(He hangs up.)*

SAM. *(Back to secretary.)* Ma'am? The chef's in a meeting but I'll have him call you as soon as he's — *(Dial tone; she's hung up. Sam moves on to a new line.)* Thank you for holding, how can I help you?

JUDITH RUSH. Hello? Hello? Who am I speaking with?

SAM. This is Sam, how can I help you?

JUDITH RUSH. Sam, I was in the restaurant last night with my two daughters and — *(As if she'd forgotten to mention it before.)* I'm a senior citizen!

SAM. Okay ...

JUDITH RUSH. And the maitre d'hotel insisted that he would take care of us, and when the bill came he charged us for everything!

SAM. *(Not quite getting it.)* He charged you for everything?

JUDITH RUSH. Yes. Evidently he thought he could take advantage of a senior citizen.

SAM. Okay, I'm not sure I understand the situation.

JUDITH RUSH. He insisted that I was not entitled to the double-A.R.P. discount!

SAM. Ohh ... well I don't think we do accept that discount.

JUDITH RUSH. *(Offended.)* I'm eighty-four years old!

SAM. No, it's not that —

JUDITH RUSH. And I've gone through a lot! Three eye operations. Cataracts in my left eye and glaucoma in both eyes. And previously I had a bladder suspension also. *(The phone rings.)*

SAM. Okay, one moment please. *(On to his new line.)* Reservations, could you hold please?

(Paramount lady — a bitter workaholic.)

PARAMOUNT LADY. I'm calling from Paramount.
SAM. I'll be right with you. *(Back to Mrs. Rush.)* I'm sorry about that, ma'am.
JUDITH RUSH. *(As if she hadn't noticed Sam was gone.)* You see, people think that an elderly person is not going to check the bill. But I did! I was in business thirty-five years as vice president of the Rush Furniture Company in Herkimer, New York —
SAM. Ma'am, why don't you give me your name and I'll ask the chef about the double-A.R.P. discount?
JUDITH RUSH. Mrs. Judith Rush.
SAM. All right. I've got your number right here. Is there anything else I can do for you?
JUDITH RUSH. *(Angling for a bigger discount.)* Well, to be honest with you, I was very disappointed in the quality of the food.
JEAN-CLAUDE. *(Buzzing in from the kitchen.)* Sam!! Sam, pick up!
SAM. I'll be right with you, Mrs. Rush. *(To Jean-Claude.)* What?
JEAN-CLAUDE. Why you didn't tell me Henry Kravis was a V.I.P.?
SAM. Jean-Claude, it says V.I.P. right by his name.
JEAN-CLAUDE. Yeah, but I didn't know who he is so I give him a table right by the kitchen door and now Mr. Hiashi tell me he's in the paper every day.
SAM. How was I supposed to know?
JEAN-CLAUDE. That's part of your job, Sam. I mean really! *(He hangs up.)*
SAM. *(Imitating Jean-Claude.)* That's part of your job, Sam. I mean, really.
OSCAR. *(Buzzing in.)* Sam, don't forget. No Ned Finlay.
SAM. *(Amused.)* Okay, thanks Oscar. *(Back to Mrs. Rush.)* I'm sorry about that, Mrs. Rush. Now where were we?
JUDITH RUSH. I was saying that I was very disappointed with the quality of the food.
SAM. I'm so sorry to hear that. What did you have?
JUDITH RUSH. We had the — *(Badly mispronounced.)* — duh-gustatation menu and frankly, I didn't care for it.
SAM. What was the problem?

JUDITH RUSH. Well, the portions were very small.

SAM. The tasting menu is designed to give you a small sample of each of the chef's specialties.

JUDITH RUSH. Well, is it designed to be cold?

SAM. No ...

JUDITH RUSH. Well, everything we ate was cold. The salmon was cold. The bread was cold, the soup was cold, the lamb was bitter cold. The deserts were scrumptious, but cold. And the coffee was freezing! We had to send everything back to be reheated.

SAM. I'm sorry you had such a bad experience.

JUDITH RUSH. *(Conspiratorial.)* Well don't forget this one last thing. At the end of the evening, I went to the powder room and I sat in a puddle of urine.

SAM. On the floor?

JUDITH RUSH. No, on the toilet seat!

SAM. You mean someone forgot to wipe the seat?

JUDITH RUSH. Yes. In a restaurant of your caliber, I thought it was terrible.

SAM. Well, I'm going to talk to the chef about it right away and I'll get back to you okay?

JUDITH RUSH. All right. Don't forget to tell him I'm a senior citizen.

SAM. I won't.

JUDITH RUSH. Okay, thank you honey. *(She hangs up. The phone rings.)*

SAM. *(On to a new line.)* Good afternoon, reservations, could you hold please?

PARAMOUNT LADY. No, I tried that before.

SAM. Okay, how can I help you?

PARAMOUNT LADY. *(Very butch.)* I'm calling from Paramount and I'd like to come in for dinner either the fifteenth, the twenty-second, or the twenty-ninth of this month.

SAM. I'm sorry, sir, we're —

PARAMOUNT LADY. *(Correcting Sam.)* Ma'am.

SAM. *(Mortified.)* I'm sorry, ma'am, we're fully committed Fridays and —

PARAMOUNT LADY. All right, second choice: Saturday the sixteenth, the twenty-third, or the thirtieth.

SAM. *(Trying to control himself.)* Actually, ma'am, right now all my weekends are fully committed through February so —

PARAMOUNT LADY. Well, it has to be one of those three weekends; those are the only times Sherry'll be in town.

SAM. Well, if you're looking for a weekend, I could either offer you the waiting list or you could call back on the first of January for a March reservation.

PARAMOUNT LADY. What a bunch of pretentious crap.

SAM. *(Taken aback.)* Ma'am, I know it's hard to make a reservation here, but I'm just doing my job.

PARAMOUNT LADY. Yeah, well why don't you go fuck yourself. *(She hangs up. Sam is stunned. He sits there for a second in a mild state of shock, disliking his job intensely. Before he can muster the strength to move, Oscar buzzes him.)*

OSCAR. *(Buzzing in.)* Sam. I forgot to ask you, how was your callback?

SAM. It was fine. Thanks for asking, Oscar. *(Sam makes a phone call.)*

CURTIS. Diana Drake Agency.

SAM. Hi Curtis, it's Sam. Is Diana there?

CURTIS. *(Bullshitting.)* She just popped into a meeting, Sam, but I gave her the message.

SAM. Curtis, have you guys been getting bad feedback about me?

CURTIS. Sam ... I know this business with HBO was disappointing, but we've been over this. They decided to go in a different direction with the role. That's all.

SAM. Well did they say why?

CURTIS. Sam, you're very talented, everyone knows you're talented ...

SAM. But?

CURTIS. But you do tend to convey a certain lack of ... entitlement.

SAM. Excuse me?

CURTIS. A sense of deserving, a sense of worthiness, a sense of status, if you will.

SAM. Have people actually said that, or is this from you?

CURTIS. *(Getting snippy.)* Sam, you asked for feedback and I gave it to you. Now if it's making you this upset, and it sounds like it is, I think you need to look within and see why it's bothering you so much. *(The phone rings.)*

SAM. Okay, thanks. *(New line.)* Good afternoon, reservations; could you hold please?

ROSENSTEIN-FISHBURN. This is Carolann Rosenstein-Fishburn calling for the third time today.

SAM. One moment please. *(Buzzing upstairs.)* Jean-Claude!!

JEAN-CLAUDE. Be brief.

SAM. Carolann Rosenstein-Fishburn on line three.

JEAN-CLAUDE. She's so ugly, Sam, you can't believe it. She has a face like a catfish.

SAM. *(Back to Mrs. Fishburn.)* Okay Mrs. Fishburn, he can't come to the phone right now, but I'll have him — *(Dial tone; she's hung up. Sam buzzes upstairs.)* Stephanie?

JEAN-CLAUDE. No, it's not Stephanie. Why are you buzzing us all day long?

SAM. Jean-Claude, can you watch the phones for like two minutes? I need to grab some food and I'm about to pee in my pants. *(The phone rings.)*

JEAN-CLAUDE. Sam, what are you — five years old? I have Mr. and Mrs. Zagat standing here waiting for a table! I can't watch the phones for nobody! *(He hangs up. The phone is still ringing.)*

SAM. *(Not pleased.)* Thanks. *(Picking up a new line.)* Reservations, can I help you?

BRYCE. Hi Sam, it's Bryce from Naomi Campbell's office, I think you forgot about me before.

SAM. I'm sorry Bryce.

BRYCE. No, I know how busy you are, but I just got out of a meeting with Naomi and we wanted to go over one last detail with you.

SAM. Okay.

BRYCE. We wanted to know how close table seventeen is to the lighting sconce.

SAM. How close?

BRYCE. Yeah. *(A beat, and then.)* Okay, when Naomi was in last time, she found the lighting a little harsh, so if table seventeen is too close to the sconce, rather than change tables, what she'd like to do is change bulbs from whatever it is you're using to something a little softer, which we would be more than happy to supply.

SAM. *(About to get testy.)* Bryce I —

BRYCE. Sam, don't worry! I'll send my assistant over and she'll take care of it. Her name is Tasha and I'll have her run over with some halogen bulbs at like five o'clock.

SAM. Okay.

BRYCE. Super, that's all for now! Thanks a gazillion! *(He hangs up. The phone rings.)*

SAM. Reservations, could you hold please?

(Steven — Sam's perfect older brother. A real straight arrow.)

STEVEN. Hey Sammy, it's Steven.

SAM. *(Doesn't ring a bell.)* Steven …

STEVEN. Your brother?

SAM. Oh Steven, I'm sorry. How are you doing?

STEVEN. Not too bad. How's it goin' with you?

SAM. It's going okay.

STEVEN. Dad told me about what happened with that HBO thing. That stinks.

SAM. Yeah, thanks.

STEVEN. Now what's this I hear about you not goin' home for Christmas?

SAM. Well, I'm trying, I just — I'm having trouble getting off from work.

STEVEN. *(Incredulous.)* You gotta work on Christmas?

SAM. Yeah, they serve Christmas dinner.

STEVEN. Sammo, I thought you were gonna get outta the restaurant business.

SAM. Yeah, I'm trying. I just —

STEVEN. Sammo, someone's gotta spend Christmas with Dad.

SAM. I thought you guys were going to be there.

STEVEN. Christine's not supposed to fly in her last trimester, remember?

SAM. Oh shit.

STEPHANIE. *(Desperate.)* Sam, pick up!!

SAM. *(To Steven.)* Steven let me call you right back.

STEVEN. Okey-doke.

STEPHANIE. Sam, please pick up!!!!!

41

SAM. *(To Stephanie.)* Yeah?

STEPHANIE. *(Very hush-hush; there are lots of customers upstairs now.)* There's been a bit of an emergency.

SAM. What, Zagat?

STEPHANIE. No, apparently a woman was taken ill in the bathroom.

SAM. *(Genuine concern.)* Ooo, is she okay?

STEPHANIE. I think she'll be all right ... but apparently she missed the toilet.

SAM. Eeew. Did she puke?

STEPHANIE. *(Trying to speak in code so the customers won't understand.)* Well it's the same principle ... but a different outlet.

SAM. *(Dawning on him.)* Eeeeeew!!

STEPHANIE. Yes! And all of the busboys are hiding. And Jean-Claude is losing his mind because Zagat still isn't seated. Sam, I know it's awful, but please would you come upstairs and — *(The phone rings.)*

SAM. Hold on, okay? *(New line.)* Reservations, could you hold please?

(Gloria Hathaway — a food critic in the midst of a long-standing feud with the Chef.)

GLORIA HATHAWAY. No, this is Gloria Hathaway calling for the chef.

SAM. Okay, one moment please. *(On to a new line.)* Reservations, could you hold please?

(Jean-Claude's wife — a big, tough French lady. Sounds a lot like Jean-Claude.)

JEAN-CLAUDE'S WIFE. I'm calling for Jean-Claude.

SAM. Could you hold please?

JEAN-CLAUDE'S WIFE. It's his wife.

SAM. One moment please. *(Sam heads to the bat phone.)* Chef? Chef!!

CHEF. I heard you the first time.

SAM. Gloria Hathaway is on line two.

CHEF. Tell her I'm in a meeting.

SAM. Okay. *(Back to Hathaway.)* Ms. Hathaway, the chef's in a meeting, is there something I can help you with?

GLORIA HATHAWAY. *(Not buying it.)* He's in a meeting?

SAM. Uh-huh. Can I take a message?

GLORIA HATHAWAY. *(Disturbed, but not out of control.)* Yeah, I have a photographer who's been waiting for him in your lounge since eight-thirty this morning and I want the chef to tell me what's going on. And you can tell him we're going have to kill the article if he can't cooperate with us. *(She hangs up.)*

STEPHANIE. *(Buzzing in.)* Sam, please! I can't leave the podium right now.

SAM. Oh Steph …

STEPHANIE. *(Desperate.)* Please, Jean-Claude is apoplectic.

SAM. *(Whimpering.)* Mmmm … *(The phone rings.)* Hold on. *(New line.)* Reservations, could you hold please?

ROSENSTEIN-FISHBURN. *(Livid.)* No, it's Carolann Rosenstein-Fishburn. Put Jean-Claude on the phone this instant!!

SAM. He's in the middle of lunch service, can I take a message?

ROSENSTEIN-FISHBURN. No, this is an emergency! I want you to tell Jean-Claude that we are entertaining a major cultural dignitary this Friday and if we do not resolve this situation right away, we will transfer all our future business to Le Bernadin!

SAM. Okay, one moment please.

JEAN-CLAUDE. *(Buzzing in.)* Sam!!

SAM. Jean-Claude, line two and line four are both for you.

JEAN-CLAUDE. Sam, you have to go to the ladies room right now!

SAM. No, I have four lines on hold —

JEAN-CLAUDE. What do you mean no?

SAM. Why can't you get a busboy?

JEAN-CLAUDE. Are you crazy? Listen Sam, we have to clean up the problem immediately in case Mrs. Zagat go in there! Do you understand?! *(The Chef buzzes in.)*

SAM. *(To Jean-Claude.)* Hold on, it's the chef. *(Sam runs to the bat phone.)* Yes, Chef?

CHEF. *(Perversely curious.)* What'd Hathaway say?

SAM. She wants to know why you've kept her photographer waiting since eight-thirty this morning.

CHEF. Yeah, well maybe she should have thought of that when she wrote that shit about my bouillabaisse.

SAM. *(Humoring him.)* Uh-huh.

CHEF. *(Very frat-boy.)* What a bitch! She's a bitch right?

SAM. *(Pretending to commiserate with Chef.)* Yeah.

CHEF. What else did she say?

SAM. She said she'll have to kill the article if you can't cooperate.

CHEF. Yeah, good. The only thing she can cooperate with is my ass. *(He hangs up.)*

JEAN-CLAUDE. *(Buzzing in, frantic.)* Sam!!! Did you clean it up?

SAM. Get a busboy. *(The phone rings.)*

JEAN-CLAUDE. Listen, no more fooling around. Mrs. Zagat just ask me, "Where is the bathroom?"!! *(The phone is still ringing.)*

SAM. Oh God … hold on. *(New line.)* Reservations, could you hold please?

DAD. Hey-a kiddo!

SAM. Hey Dad. How ya doin'?

DAD. I'm okay kiddo. Just wanted to see if ya talked to the big guy yet.

SAM. Yeah, it doesn't look too good.

DAD. *(Covering his disappointment.)* Oh well, that's okay.

SAM. I'm sorry Dad.

DAD. No that's okay, amigo. You gotta work, you gotta work.

SAM. I just — what are you gonna do for Christmas dinner?

DAD. Don't worry about me kid. I'm okay. I can go to your uncle Carl's or a whole bunch of other places. You need anything kid? You okay for cash?

SAM. No, I'm fine. *(The Chef buzzes in.)* Dad, I've got to go. Let me call you back a little later.

DAD. All right then. Adios amigo! *(He hangs up.)*

SAM. Adios. *(More buzzing. Sam heads to the bat phone. Dreading this.)* Yes, Chef?

CHEF. *(Out of control.)* What the fuck is going on down there? Jean-Claude just told me you refused to go to the ladies room?

SAM. I didn't refuse, I just —

CHEF. What kind of horseshit is that? Mrs. Zagat is on her way down the hall.

SAM. Chef, I —

CHEF. Sam, I'm not asking you, I'm telling you okay???

SAM. Chef, that's not part of my job.

CHEF. It's not part of your job? Sam, your job is to do whatever I goddamn tell you to. And right now I'm telling you to get into that fucking bathroom.

SAM. I don't understand why you can't get a busboy.

CHEF. You don't need to understand, Sam. Just get up here and clean it up! *(Sam stands up and exits.)*

(Blackout — during which time we hear overwrought classical music, phones ringing out of whack, and snippets of Jean-Claude's conversation upstairs in the lounge.)

JEAN-CLAUDE. *(Manic.)* **Sam! Sam! What line is my wife on? Allo? Allo! Stephanie, please get Mr. Zagat a martini or something. Luis, please check on table thirty-one and see what the delay is.** *(Then suddenly.)* **Mrs. Zagat? Where are you going? To the ladies room? So soon? I mean we hardly even started our conversation. I don't know how you doing, how the little Zagats are doing or anything.** *(A beat.)* **Okay, I see you in a minute.** *(Wild cursing in French.)* **Luis, qu'est-que ce passe? Where is the goddamn busboy?** *Putain!* *(Desperately buzzing Sam.)* **Sam! Sam! Sam!** *(A moment of silence in the dark, followed by a big flushing sound. Then, an envelope comes flying down the stairs. Lights up again on Sam, walking back down into the reservation office, trauma-stricken after his experience in the bathroom. He picks up the envelope, but before he can open it, the intercom buzzes. Still buzzing.)* **Sam! Sam! Sam!**

SAM. Yes?

JEAN-CLAUDE. Did you get to the ladies room in time?

SAM. Yup.

JEAN-CLAUDE. Oh wonderful, I got the Zagat table ready right now. Everything's under control. *(He hangs up. The phone rings.)*

SAM. Reservations, how can I help you?

(Smarmy Man — a real smooth operator.)

SMARMY MAN. *(Singing.)* "Deck the halls with boughs of holly!"

SAM. How can I help you?

SMARMY MAN. *(Still singing.)* "Fa-la-la-la-la la-la la la!"

SAM. One moment please. *(He puts him on hold for a beat, then returns.)* Thank you for holding, how can I help you?

SMARMY MAN. Thank you for being there. Who'm I speaking to?

SAM. Sam.

SMARMY MAN. Sam. Sammy. The Samster. Whaddaya have for me this weekend?

SAM. I'm sorry, sir. We're fully committed this weekend.

SMARMY MAN. Whoa-whoa! Samster, what's the matter?

SAM. Nothing, is there something else I can help you —

SMARMY MAN. No, something's wrong, Samster. What's goin' on?

SAM. *(Letting his guard down, a moment of real honesty.)* Just a bad day.

SMARMY MAN. *(Sympathetic.)* Hey Samster, don't let the big guys getcha down.

SAM. Okay …

SMARMY MAN. You're number one! You're the man. Sam the man.

SAM. Okay …

SMARMY MAN. *(Singing.)* "Joy to the world, the Lord has — "

SAM. *(Reaching his breaking point.)* Okay-okay-okay. How can I help you?

SMARMY MAN. How about Saturday at eight o'clock?

SAM. *(A beat.)* How about ten o'clock?

SMARMY MAN. Bee-autiful.

SAM. Last name.

SMARMY MAN. Finlay.

SAM. First name?

SMARMY MAN. Ned.

SAM. Okay, Ned. We'll see you on Saturday. Jacket and tie for men, okay?

SMARMY MAN. Of course! Now you hang in there, Samster. *(He hangs up. Sam suddenly remembers where he's seen the name Ned Finlay. He lunges for the phone to try and reverse the damage. No luck.)*

HECTOR. *(Buzzing in from the kitchen.)* Hey, Papi. They told me what happened to you. That's disgusting.

SAM. Yeah. *(The phone rings.)*

HECTOR. You want me to make you some food?

SAM. No thanks, Hector. *(Picking up the line.)* Reservations, could you hold please?

(Nancy — Bob's girlfriend.)

NANCY. Hi Sam, it's Nancy.

SAM. *(Desperate.)* Nancy, where is Bob?

NANCY. I guess he's still at Bed Bath and Beyond.

SAM. Bed Bath and Beyond?

NANCY. Didn't he tell you Sam? He has an interview today.

SAM. Oh right ...

NANCY. Have him call me as soon as he gets back.

SAM. I sure will. *(Buzzing upstairs.)* Stephanie.

STEPHANIE. Oh Sam, I'm so sorry; it must have been awful.

SAM. No, it's not even that. Bob's little girlfriend just called and told me that he's been on a job interview all day.

STEPHANIE. No! *(The bat phone buzzes.)*

SAM. I'm just — hold on. *(Sam heads to the bat phone.)* Yes, Chef?

CHEF. *(Perversely curious.)* Was it gross?

SAM. Yes, it was gross.

CHEF. *(Laughing.)* Oh man, I can't believe you did it. *(The phone rings.)*

SAM. Yeah, well, I did it. *(Sam hangs up on the Chef and picks up the phone.)* Reservations, could you hold please?

BOB. Hey Sam, it's Bob. How you holdin' up?

SAM. *(Fit to be tied.)* Where are you?

BOB. I'm about two minutes away. Nancy's takin' me in.

SAM. That's funny, because she just called to see how your interview went.

BOB. *(Starting to sweat.)* I don't know what you're talking about.

SAM. *(Having fun.)* Really? Well I hope you do know something about Mr. Zagat's lunch reservation. I believe he said he confirmed it with you, but when he showed up he wasn't even on the list! It's

47

been causing quite a ruckus around here.

BOB. Sam, I really don't like the tone you're taking with me.

SAM. Really? Well maybe you'd prefer to talk to the chef.

BOB. Sam, don't — *(Sam hangs up on Bob and heads to the bat phone.)*

SAM. Chef, Bob's on line two.

CHEF. Well goody-goody gumdrops. *(The phone rings.)*

SAM. Reservations, could you hold please?

CURTIS. Surprise, surprise. Guess who got a second callback at Lincoln Center?

SAM. *(Ecstatic.)* Oh my God — Curtis!

CURTIS. Tomorrow morning at ten-thirty.

SAM. Oh my God!

CURTIS. Talk to you later, Sam.

SAM. Do I need to prepare anything?

CURTIS. Just a strong sense of personal entitlement. Toodle-oo. *(He hangs up.)*

SAM. *(Buzzing Stephanie.)* Steph, I got the callback!

STEPHANIE. Oh Sam! Congratulations!

SAM. *(To Stephanie.)* I can't believe it. *(The Chef buzzes in.)* Hold on, it's the chef. *(Sam runs to the bat phone.)* Yes, Chef?

CHEF. What time do I need to be at the heliport?

SAM. *(He completely spaced the helicopter.)* I think it's in half an hour. Let me just double check. *(To himself.)* Shit. *(Sam runs back to his desk and rifles through the rolodex. The phone rings. Sam picks up.)* Reservations, could you hold please?

JERRY. Hey babe, it's Jerry.

SAM. Hey Jerry, what's up?

JERRY. Sam, you're not going to believe this!!

SAM. What?

JERRY. I just booked a national spot for Taco Bell!

SAM. That's great. Congratulations.

JERRY. I can't believe it! I mean I really feel like I'm on a roll. Hey! Congratulations to you too. Curtis told me you got the callback.

SAM. Yeah, thanks.

JERRY. I just came back from mine two minutes ago.

SAM. How'd it go?

JERRY. Unbelievable! I mean, I really feel like I've begun to develop a relationship with the people up there. Oh God, Sam. It's so weird what we put ourselves through. Years and years of training and in the end, it's all about connections, isn't it? *(The Chef buzzes in on the bat phone.)*

SAM. Jerry, I have to go.

JERRY. All right, well let's keep talking. I think it's really great that we're being so honest with one another. *(The Chef continues to buzz.)*

SAM. Yeah, me too. *(Sam hangs up and rushes to the bat phone.)* Yes, Chef?

CHEF. Did you find out?

SAM. I'm just double-checking right now.

CHEF. Shouldn't you have done that about six hours ago? *(He hangs up. Sam looks through the rolodex and dials a number.)*

(Rick from Carson Aviation — the kind of unflappable, even-keeled guy you want to have behind the controls of an airplane.)

RICK FROM CARSON AVIATION. Carson Aviation.

SAM. Hi, this is Sam from Bob Walker's office. Who am I speaking with?

RICK FROM CARSON AVIATION. This is Rick.

SAM. Rick, Bob asked me to call and confirm the chef's six o'clock departure tonight.

RICK FROM CARSON AVIATION. *(Looking at his log sheets.)* Okay, Sam, let me call that up for you, one second. Okay, I see the account, but I don't see anything in there about tonight's order.

SAM. *(Starting to cop an attitude.)* What do you mean?

RICK FROM CARSON AVIATION. Now hold on, do you remember who he confirmed it with?

SAM. Yeah, we confirmed it with you like two weeks ago.

RICK FROM CARSON AVIATION. You did huh? Well I don't see it —

SAM. *(Working himself into a state.)* I can't believe this. The chef's supposed to leave in half an hour!

RICK. Now hold on there — *(Suddenly, an emergency operator breaks through the line.)*

49

EMERGENCY OPERATOR. *(Computer-generated voice.)* Hello, this is … *(James Earl Jones-like voice.)* Bell Atlantic *(Back to computer.)* … with an emergency breakthrough for Sam.

SAM. *(Genuinely worried.)* This is Sam.

ROSENSTEIN-FISHBURN. It is Carolann Rosenstein-Fishburn calling for the tenth time today.

SAM. Is there an emergency?

ROSENSTEIN-FISHBURN. Yes, there most certainly is. Put Jean-Claude on the phone this instant.

SAM. *(Exasperated.)* Mrs. Fishburn, Jean-Claude's in the middle of service, but he'll call you as soon as he's done, okay?

ROSENSTEIN-FISHBURN. I am not hanging up until you put him on the phone.

SAM. Hold on for one second.

ROSENSTEIN-FISHBURN. I'll hold all day.

SAM. *(Buzzing upstairs.)* Jean-Claude!! Carolann Fishburn on line three.

JEAN-CLAUDE. Sam, she's so ugly.

SAM. *(Back to Mrs. Fishburn.)* Mrs. Fishburn, he can't come to the phone right now.

ROSENSTEIN-FISHBURN. I know he's there and I'm not hanging up until you put him on this phone.

SAM. Well, he's still busy, but you are welcome to hold on for as long as you like.

ROSENSTEIN-FISHBURN. Okay, I will.

SAM. Okay, good. *(The phone rings.)* Reservations, could you hold please?

RICK FROM CARSON AVIATION. Sam, it's Rick at Carson Aviation. I think we got cut off before. Sorry about all the confusion. Just wanted to let you know I'm checking into the situation and I'll be back to you in five.

SAM. Thanks, Rick. *(Sam picks up a stray line.)* How ya doing there?

ROSENSTEIN-FISHBURN. I am not hanging up until you put him on the phone.

SAM. *(Perversely sensitive.)* I know, I'm just checking in. *(The phone rings.)* Reservations, how can I help you?

(Mr. Decoste — the mysterious stranger.)

MR. DECOSTE. Sam, how are you?

SAM. Good, how are you?

MR. DECOSTE. Did you get my package?

SAM. No, I don't — *(Remembering the envelope.)* Oh yeah … I did get it. *(Sam opens the envelope.)*

MR. DECOSTE. And? *(Sam pulls out a huge wad of cash.)*

SAM. *(Deadpan.)* When would you like to come in?

MR. DECOSTE. How about seven-thirty?

SAM. And your last name?

MR. DECOSTE. Decoste.

SAM. And how many?

MR. DECOSTE. Two.

SAM. We'll see you tonight at seven-thirty.

MR. DECOSTE. Thank you Sam. *(He hangs up. Sam buzzes upstairs as fast as he can.)*

SAM. *(Buzzing upstairs.)* Jean-Claude?

JEAN-CLAUDE. *(Testy.)* Yes, you don't need to scream, I can hear you.

SAM. Bob left a name off tonight's list. *(Sheepishly looking around.)* It's Decoste at seven-thirty. Party of two. And he's a V.I.P.

JEAN-CLAUDE. *(Thick with sarcasm.)* Oh he's a V.I.P.? That's wonderful. I'm so happy for him. *(He hangs up. The bat phone rings. Sam rushes to pick it up.)*

SAM. Yes, Chef?

CHEF. What time do I need to be ready?

SAM. I'm not sure yet, the line's busy.

CHEF. Jesus Christ. *(He hangs up.)*

JEAN-CLAUDE. *(Buzzing in.)* Sam! Pick up!

SAM. *(To Jean-Claude.)* Yes?

JEAN-CLAUDE. *(Sucking up.)* Listen, you silly-billy, you need to do a really big favor for me, okay? Remember we took a special request for the Veccini table at five? *(Dripping with charm.)* Well, it's so funny because I'm asking all the waiters, do they know the words to the song "Lady is the Tramp" and nobody seem to heard of it before. So I —

SAM. No way.

JEAN-CLAUDE. Oh Sam, come on, you supposed to be an actor. It's good experience, you never know, maybe the guy has connections in the movie business.

SAM. Jean —

JEAN-CLAUDE. Oh Sam, it's just going to take one minute. I thought you were my buddy.

SAM. No, I'm —

JEAN-CLAUDE. Oh forget it! I mean if you were really an actor you wouldn't be answering phones all day now would you? *(He hangs up. Stung, Sam picks up a spare line. He's not sure who's there.)*

SAM. Thank you for holding, how can I help you?

ROSENSTEIN-FISHBURN. It is Carolann Rosen —

SAM. Oh right. *(Suddenly taking charge.)* You know what, Carolann ... Jean-Claude has left for the day.

ROSENSTEIN-FISHBURN. You have got to be kidding.

SAM. *(Losing patience.)* No I'm not. Why don't you just put your name on our waiting list for Friday and call it a day.

ROSENSTEIN-FISHBURN. *(Through clenched teeth.)* All right, you little snot, put me in the first slot on the V.I.P. priority waiting list. Party of six. And why don't you put it under the name of our guest of honor — Bernard Gersten. Maybe you've heard of him. He's the executive producer of Lincoln Center.

SAM. *(A beat.)* Actually, I have heard of him.

ROSENSTEIN-FISHBURN. Is that so?

SAM. *(Testing the waters.)* Yeah, it's so funny that you should mention his name because I'm actually up for a part in a show at Lincoln Center.

ROSENSTEIN-FISHBURN. *(She's biting.)* Really?

SAM. Uh-huh. In fact, I'm going back for a callback tomorrow morning.

ROSENSTEIN-FISHBURN. Well Sam, that is funny because I just got off the phone with Bernie and I happen to know that there's nothing he loves more than the opportunity to help out a struggling young actor.

SAM. Really?

ROSENSTEIN-FISHBURN. Oh yes.

SAM. *(Enjoying this.)* You know what Carolann, I can't believe I overlooked this before. I just happened to notice that a table opened up on Friday night.

ROSENSTEIN-FISHBURN. Really? At what time?

SAM. Ten o'clock.

ROSENSTEIN-FISHBURN. Eight o'clock.

SAM. Nine-thirty.

ROSENSTEIN-FISHBURN. Eight-thirty.

SAM. Nine o'clock.

ROSENSTEIN-FISHBURN. That's tremendous. And your last name Sam?

SAM. Peliczowski.

ROSENSTEIN-FISHBURN. Marvelous. I'll call Bernie right now. And Sam, we'll need table thirty-one.

SAM. Shouldn't be a problem. *(The phone rings. Sam picks up the new line.)* Reservations, could you hold please?

RICK FROM CARSON AVIATION. Sam, it's Rick from Carson Aviation. I can't seem to figure out what happened to your record, but I got a Sicorski here and I'm gonna take her out myself. We'll send a car for him in about twenty-five.

SAM. Thank you, Rick.

BOB. *(Buzzing in from upstairs.)* Sam! Sam, it's Bob.

SAM. Where are you?

BOB. *(Whispering.)* I'm upstairs.

SAM. Get down here! I want to go home.

BOB. Look Sam, I'll be down in two seconds. I just want to wait till the chef leaves. I don't want him to see me.

SAM. I thought you had a job at Bed Bath and Beyond.

BOB. To tell you the truth Sam, the interview didn't go that well so I'd really appreciate it if you didn't mention it to the chef.

SAM. Really? Well I hope you won't mind if I make a few little schedule changes.

BOB. Yeah-yeah. Whatever you want Sam.

SAM. I remembered that you wanted to pick up a few extra shifts, so I'm gonna put you down for mine on the twenty-fourth and twenty-fifth.

BOB. Whatever … Hey wait a minute, that's Christmas!

SAM. Yes it is. *(The Chef buzzes in on the bat phone. Sam picks up.)* Yes, Chef?

CHEF. *(Livid.)* When the fuck is my car coming?

SAM. Twenty-five minutes.

CHEF. *(Calming down.)* Oh. Cool. *(A beat.)* Hey Sam — do your hands smell like shit?

SAM. No they don't.

CHEF. *(Cracking up.)* I can't believe I made you do that.

SAM. Me either.

CHEF. I owe you, Sam. You want some food? I could make you some orange roughy that'll bring you to your knees.

SAM. *(A beat.)* You know what Chef, I don't really care for your orange roughy.

CHEF. *(A beat.)* What did you just say?

SAM. It's actually one of your weaker dishes.

CHEF. *(Floored.)* Are you serious?

SAM. Yeah, I am.

CHEF. *(Cowed.)* Do you like my polenta? *(The phone rings.)*

SAM. *(To Chef.)* Yeah, it's okay. Hold on. *(Sam hangs up on Chef and picks up new line.)* Reservations, how can I help you?

CURTIS. Sam, Curtis. You're not going to believe this.

SAM. What?

CURTIS. Diana just came back from a meeting at Lincoln Center and she was talking you up, so much so, that Bernard Gersten himself wants you to stop in and say hi after your audition. *(A beat.)* See Sam, we're always working for you, even when you think we're not. *(He hangs up. The Chef buzzes. Sam heads to the bat phone.)*

SAM. Yes, Chef?

CHEF. How do you feel about my apple strudel?

SAM. *(Sincere.)* Oh, it's excellent.

CHEF. *(Wounded.)* You're just saying that to be nice. *(The phones start to go nuts.)*

SAM. No, I'm not. I really like it. Ask Stephanie.

CHEF. All right, I will. *(Just for the fun of it, Sam picks up his headset and starts grabbing the various lines.)*

SAM. Reservations, could you hold please?

BRYCE. Yeah it's Bryce, I'll hold!!!

SAM. Reservations, could you hold please?

(Mr. Inoue — a Japanese business executive.)

INOUE. My name is Inoue. "I" as in Eiffel Tower —
SAM. *(New line.)* Reservations, could you hold please?
MRS. VANDEVERE. Sam, it's Mrs. Vandevere.
SAM. *(New line.)* Reservations, could you hold please?

(Dr. Ruth Westheimer.)

DR. RUTH. Hello, this is Dr. Ruth Westheimer!
SAM. *(New line.)* Reservations, could you hold please?
SEBAG. Herbert, it's Mrs. Sebag!!
SAM. One moment please.
OSCAR. *(Buzzing in.)* Sam.
SAM. Yes, Oscar.
OSCAR. I heard about your callback. Break a leg.
SAM. Thanks, Oscar. *(Sam takes a beat, then dials a number.)*
JERRY'S MACHINE. **This is Jerry Miller at 499-3210. Your call is really important to me. Please leave a message and I'll get right back to you.**
SAM. Hey Jerry, it's Sam. *(Playing dumb.)* Listen, I just found out I'm supposed to pop my head in Bernard Gersten's office when I go up there tomorrow. I don't know what that's all about, but I just wanted to fill you in because I know it's really important to you for us to be honest. *(He hangs up.)*
JEAN-CLAUDE. *(Buzzing in.)* Sam!!
SAM. *(Calm.)* Yes.
JEAN-CLAUDE. I can't believe you leaving me in the lurch. The Veccinis are finishing their strudel.
SAM. I thought you said forget about it.
JEAN-CLAUDE. *(Abject.)* I was kidding Sam! What do you want me to get down on my hands and knees??!!!
SAM. Well, didn't we charge them $295 for this?
JEAN-CLAUDE. Oh Sam, you so greedy!
SAM. Is that a yes or a no?
JEAN-CLAUDE. Yes-yes-yes!! What are you waiting for?
SAM. I'll be right there. *(Sam dials another number.)*
DAD'S MACHINE. **Hey, it's Jack. I can't get to the phone right**

now so leave me a message at the beep tone.

SAM. *(Into the machine.)* Hey Dad, it's Sam. Are you there? Okay, well ... I just wanted to let you know there's been a little change of plans and I'm going to go ahead and make that reservation after all — okay. I'll talk to you later. *(Sam hangs up and starts gathering his things, singing a few bars of "The Lady is a Tramp" as he heads up the spiral staircase. The bat phone buzzes. Sam turns around for a moment, and considers picking it up, then decides against it and continues his ascent, singing as he rushes up and out.)*

The End

PROPERTY LIST

Headset
Old menu
Message pad
Envelope with money
Rolodex

SOUND EFFECTS

Phones ringing
Buzzer
Dial tone
Chef's special phone buzz
Sounds of a busy restaurant
Overwrought classical music
Big flushing sound
Recorded voices
Answering machine beeps

NEW PLAYS

★ **HONOUR by Joanna Murray-Smith.** In a series of intense confrontations, a wife, husband, lover and daughter negotiate the forces of passion, history, responsibility and honour. "HONOUR makes for surprisingly interesting viewing. Tight, crackling dialogue (usually played out in punchy verbal duels) captures characters unable to deal with emotions ... Murray-Smith effectively places her characters in situations that strip away pretense." –*Variety* "... the play's virtues are strong: a distinctive theatrical voice, passionate concerns ... HONOUR might just capture a few honors of its own." –*Time Out Magazine* [1M, 3W] ISBN: 0-8222-1683-3

★ **MR. PETERS' CONNECTIONS by Arthur Miller.** Mr. Miller describes the protagonist as existing in a dream-like state when the mind is "freed to roam from real memories to conjectures, from trivialities to tragic insights, from terror of death to glorying in one's being alive." With this memory play, the Tony Award and Pulitzer Prize-winner reaffirms his stature as the world's foremost dramatist. "... a cross between Joycean stream-of-consciousness and Strindberg's dream plays, sweetened with a dose of William Saroyan's philosophical whimsy ... CONNECTIONS is most intriguing ..." –*The NY Times* [5M, 3W] ISBN: 0-8222-1687-6

★ **THE WAITING ROOM by Lisa Loomer.** Three women from different centuries meet in a doctor's waiting room in this dark comedy about the timeless quest for beauty – and its cost. "... THE WAITING ROOM ... is a bold, risky melange of conflicting elements that is ... terrifically moving ... There's no resisting the fierce emotional pull of the play." –*The NY Times* "... one of the high points of this year's Off-Broadway season ... THE WAITING ROOM is well worth a visit." –*Back Stage* [7M, 4W, flexible casting] ISBN: 0-8222-1594-2

★ **THE OLD SETTLER by John Henry Redwood.** A sweet-natured comedy about two church-going sisters in 1943 Harlem and the handsome young man who rents a room in their apartment. "For all of its decent sentiments, THE OLD SETTLER avoids sentimentality. It has the authenticity and lack of pretense of an Early American sampler." –*The NY Times* "We've had some fine plays Off-Broadway this season, and this is one of the best." –*The NY Post* [1M, 3W] ISBN: 0-8-222-1642-6

★ **LAST TRAIN TO NIBROC by Arlene Hutton.** In 1940 two young strangers share a seat on a train bound east only to find their paths will cross again. "All aboard. LAST TRAIN TO NIBROC is a sweetly told little chamber romance." –*Show Business* "... [a] gently charming little play, reminiscent of Thornton Wilder in its look at rustic Americans who are to be treasured for their simplicity and directness ..." –*Associated Press* "The old formula of boy wins girls, boy loses girl, boy wins girl still works ... [a] well-made play that perfectly captures a slice of small-town-life-gone-by." –*Back Stage* [1M, 1W] ISBN: 0-8222-1753-8

★ **OVER THE RIVER AND THROUGH THE WOODS by Joe DiPietro.** Nick sees both sets of his grandparents every Sunday for dinner. This is routine until he has to tell them that he's been offered a dream job in Seattle. The news doesn't sit so well. "A hilarious family comedy that is even funnier than his long running musical revue *I Love You, You're Perfect, Now Change.*" –*Back Stage* "Loaded with laughs every step of the way." –*Star-Ledger* [3M, 3W] ISBN: 0-8222-1712-0

★ **SIDE MAN by Warren Leight.** 1999 Tony Award winner. This is the story of a broken family and the decline of jazz as popular entertainment. "... a tender, deeply personal memory play about the turmoil in the family of a jazz musician as his career crumbles at the dawn of the age of rock-and-roll ..." –*The NY Times* "[SIDE MAN] is an elegy for two things – a lost world and a lost love. When the two notes sound together in harmony, it is moving and graceful ..." –*The NY Daily News* "An atmospheric memory play ... with crisp dialogue and clearly drawn characters ... reflects the passing of an era with persuasive insight ... The joy and despair of the musicians is skillfully illustrated." –*Variety* [5M, 3W] ISBN: 0-8222-1721-X

DRAMATISTS PLAY SERVICE, INC.
440 Park Avenue South, New York, NY 10016 212-683-8960 Fax 212-213-1539
postmaster@dramatists.com www.dramatists.com

NEW PLAYS

★ **CLOSER by Patrick Marber.** Winner of the 1998 Olivier Award for Best Play and the 1999 New York Drama Critics Circle Award for Best Foreign Play. Four lives intertwine over the course of four and a half years in this densely plotted, stinging look at modern love and betrayal. "CLOSER is a sad, savvy, often funny play that casts a steely, unblinking gaze at the world of relationships and lets you come to your own conclusions ... CLOSER does not merely hold your attention; it burrows into you." –*New York Magazine* "A powerful, darkly funny play about the cosmic collision between the sun of love and the comet of desire." –*Newsweek Magazine* [2M, 2W] ISBN: 0-8222-1722-8

★ **THE MOST FABULOUS STORY EVER TOLD by Paul Rudnick.** A stage manager, headset and prompt book at hand, brings the house lights to half, then dark, and cues the creation of the world. Throughout the play, she's in control of everything. In other words, she's either God, or she thinks she is. "Line by line, Mr. Rudnick may be the funniest writer for the stage in the United States today ... One-liners, epigrams, withering put-downs and flashing repartee: These are the candles that Mr. Rudnick lights instead of cursing the darkness ... a testament to the virtues of laughing ... and in laughter, there is something like the memory of Eden." –*The NY Times* "Funny it is ... consistently, rapaciously, deliriously ... easily the funniest play in town." –*Variety* [4M, 5W] ISBN: 0-8222-1720-1

★ **A DOLL'S HOUSE by Henrik Ibsen, adapted by Frank McGuinness.** Winner of the 1997 Tony Award for Best Revival. "New, raw, gut-twisting and gripping. Easily the hottest drama this season." –*USA Today* "Bold, brilliant and alive." –*The Wall Street Journal* "A thunderclap of an evening that takes your breath away." –*Time Magazine* [4M, 4W, 2 boys] ISBN: 0-8222-1636-1

★ **THE HERBAL BED by Peter Whelan.** The play is based on actual events which occurred in Stratford-upon-Avon in the summer of 1613, when William Shakespeare's elder daughter was publicly accused of having a sexual liaison with a married neighbor and family friend. "In his probing new play, THE HERBAL BED ... Peter Whelan muses about a sidelong event in the life of Shakespeare's family and creates a finely textured tapestry of love and lies in the early 17th-century Stratford." –*The NY Times* "It is a first rate drama with interesting moral issues of truth and expediency." –*The NY Post* [5M, 3W] ISBN: 0-8222-1675-2

★ **SNAKEBIT by David Marshall Grant.** A study of modern friendship when put to the test. "... a rather smart and absorbing evening of water-cooler theater, the intimate sort of Off-Broadway experience that has you picking apart the recognizable characters long after the curtain calls." –*The NY Times* "Off-Broadway keeps on presenting us with compelling reasons for going to the theater. The latest is SNAKEBIT, David Marshall Grant's smart new comic drama about being thirtysomething and losing one's way in life." –*The NY Daily News* [3M, 1W] ISBN: 0-8222-1724-4

★ **A QUESTION OF MERCY by David Rabe.** The Obie Award-winning playwright probes the sensitive and controversial issue of doctor-assisted suicide in the age of AIDS in this poignant drama. "There are many devastating ironies in Mr. Rabe's beautifully considered, piercingly clear-eyed work ..." –*The NY Times* "With unsettling candor and disturbing insight, the play arouses pity and understanding of a troubling subject ... Rabe's provocative tale is an affirmation of dignity that rings clear and true." –*Variety* [6M, 1W] ISBN: 0-8222-1643-4

★ **DIMLY PERCEIVED THREATS TO THE SYSTEM by Jon Klein.** Reality and fantasy overlap with hilarious results as this unforgettable family attempts to survive the nineties. "Here's a play whose point about fractured families goes to the heart, mind – and ears." –*The Washington Post* "... an end-of-the millennium comedy about a family on the verge of a nervous breakdown ... Trenchant and hilarious ..." –*The Baltimore Sun* [2M, 4W] ISBN: 0-8222-1677-9

DRAMATISTS PLAY SERVICE, INC.
440 Park Avenue South, New York, NY 10016 212-683-8960 Fax 212-213-1539
postmaster@dramatists.com www.dramatists.com

NEW PLAYS

★ **AS BEES IN HONEY DROWN by Douglas Carter Beane.** Winner of the John Gassner Playwriting Award. A hot young novelist finds the subject of his new screenplay in a New York socialite who leads him into the world of *Auntie Mame* and *Breakfast at Tiffany's*, before she takes him for a ride. "A delicious soufflé of a satire ... [an] extremely entertaining fable for an age that always chooses image over substance." *–The NY Times* "... A witty assessment of one of the most active and relentless industries in a consumer society ... the creation of 'hot' young things, which the media have learned to mass produce with efficiency and zeal." *–The NY Daily News* [3M, 3W, flexible casting] ISBN: 0-8222-1651-5

★ **STUPID KIDS by John C. Russell.** In rapid, highly stylized scenes, the story follows four high-school students as they make their way from first through eighth period and beyond, struggling with the fears, frustrations, and longings peculiar to youth. "In STUPID KIDS ... playwright John C. Russell gets the opera of adolescence to a T ... The stylized teenspeak of STUPID KIDS ... suggests that Mr. Russell may have hidden a tape recorder under a desk in study hall somewhere and then scoured the tapes for good quotations ... it is the kids' insular, ceaselessly churning world, a pre-adult world of Doritos and libidos, that the playwright seeks to lay bare." *–The NY Times* "STUPID KIDS [is] a sharp-edged ... whoosh of teen angst and conformity anguish. It is also very funny." *–NY Newsday* [2M, 2W] ISBN: 0-8222-1698-1

★ **COLLECTED STORIES by Donald Margulies.** From Obie Award-winner Donald Margulies comes a provocative analysis of a student-teacher relationship that turns sour when the protégé becomes a rival. "With his fine ear for detail, Margulies creates an authentic, insular world, and he gives equal weight to the opposing viewpoints of two formidable characters." *–The LA Times* "This is probably Margulies' best play to date ..." *–The NY Post* "... always fluid and lively, the play is thick with ideas, like a stock-pot of good stew." *–The Village Voice* [2W] ISBN: 0-8222-1640-X

★ **FREEDOMLAND by Amy Freed.** An overdue showdown between a son and his father sets off fireworks that illuminate the neurosis, rage and anxiety of one family – and of America at the turn of the millennium. "FREEDOMLAND's more obvious links are to *Buried Child* and *Bosoms and Neglect*. Freed, like Guare, is an inspired wordsmith with a gift for surreal touches in situations grounded in familiar and real territory." *–Curtain Up* [3M, 4W] ISBN: 0-8222-1719-8

★ **STOP KISS by Diana Son.** A poignant and funny play about the ways, both sudden and slow, that lives can change irrevocably. "There's so much that is vital and exciting about STOP KISS ... you want to embrace this young author and cheer her onto other works ... the writing on display here is funny and credible ... you also will be charmed by its heartfelt characters and up-to-the-minute humor." *–The NY Daily News* "... irresistibly exciting ... a sweet, sad, and enchantingly sincere play." *–The NY Times* [3M, 3W] ISBN: 0-8222-1731-7

★ **THREE DAYS OF RAIN by Richard Greenberg.** The sins of fathers and mothers make for a bittersweet elegy in this poignant and revealing drama. "... a work so perfectly judged it heralds the arrival of a major playwright ... Greenberg is extraordinary." *–The NY Daily News* "Greenberg's play is filled with graceful passages that are by turns melancholy, harrowing, and often, quite funny." *–Variety* [2M, 1W] ISBN: 0-8222-1676-0

★ **THE WEIR by Conor McPherson.** In a bar in rural Ireland, the local men swap spooky stories in an attempt to impress a young woman from Dublin who recently moved into a nearby "haunted" house. However, the tables are soon turned when she spins a yarn of her own. "You shed all sense of time at this beautiful and devious new play." *–The NY Times* "Sheer theatrical magic. I have rarely been so convinced that I have just seen a modern classic. Tremendous." *–The London Daily Telegraph* [4M, 1W] ISBN: 0-8222-1706-6

DRAMATISTS PLAY SERVICE, INC.
440 Park Avenue South, New York, NY 10016 212-683-8960 Fax 212-213-1539
postmaster@dramatists.com www.dramatists.com